THE
VIETNAM WAR

THE VIETNAM WAR

VOLUME 5

River War

Marshall Cavendish
New York · London · Toronto · Sydney

Reference Edition 1988

© Marshall Cavendish Limited 1988
© DPM Services Limited 1988

Published by Marshall Cavendish Corporation
             147 West Merrick Road
             Freeport
             Long Island
             N.Y. 11520

Produced by Ravelin Limited
Original text by Barry Gregory
Designed by Graham Beehag

Library of Congress Cataloging-in-Publication Data

The Vietnam War

   1. Vietnamese Conflict. 1961-1975 – United States.
I. Marshall Cavendish Corporation.
DS558.W37   1988   959.704'33'73 87-18224
ISBN 0-86307-852-4 (set)
      0-86307-858-2 (Vol 5)

Contents

Vietnam 1954-1975

Sharp Encounter

The monsoon was about to bring a deluge of rain to the Mekong Delta. It was late October 1966 and ramshackle river craft of every description thronged the Mekong waterways. The vessels ranged from crude oriental craft to the more picturesque junks, sampans and ocean-going cargo vessels.

As dusk approached on October 31st, two American patrol boats, PBRs 105 and 107, with Boatswain's Mate First Class J.E. Williams as patrol officer were conducting a special patrol near Ngo Hiep Island in the Mekong where the Viet Cong were known to have a well-established route into Kien Hoa Province to the south.

This was more than a routine river patrol. The time of year had arrived when the Viet Cong would leave their hiding places in regions like the Plain of Reeds before the rains washed them away. Commander River Division 33 had ordered a 24-hour patrol of the Ngo Hiep area and soon it would be dark.

A sampan was suddenly sighted heading out of the Nam Thon River on the northern edge of the island. The small vessel immediately aroused suspicion as civilian traffic on the Mekong waterways was prohibited during the hours of darkness. The two American patrol boats closed in pursuit.

As the sampan darted out of the flooded rice paddies, shots were aimed at PBR 105. A second sampan appeared, opened fire on the PBRs, which responded with .50-caliber machine-gun fire. The occupants of the sampans dropped their rifles and jumped into the water but they were killed before they could reach the shore.

Williams now spotted a junk and several more sampans. Because of the high tide and flood conditions, the PBRs could see the sampans actually sailing across the rice paddies on the island. The

patrol entered the Nam Thon River and immediately came under fire from the north bank and from two large junks in the inlet.

Eight small sampans, with eight to ten green-uniformed men in each boat, were seen astern of the junks. Fire from the PBRs sank two of the sampans and their survivors took to the brush. The remaining sampans took cover in the dense woods along the banks. The patrol boats cautiously withdrew along the southern edge of a small island in the Nam Thon.

Petty Officer Williams sensed there was big trouble in store and his intuition proved right when the PBRs came across a whole fleet

of sampans and junks. Some were beached and Viet Cong were disembarking from others. The guerrillas were obviously in a hurry to get away. PBRs 105 and 107 opened fire and Williams called on the radio for helicopter support from Vinh Long.

The patrol boats now withdrew to the eastern edge of Ngo Hiep to await Huey helicopter gunships appearing within 15 minutes. Upon arrival of the aerial fire team, the PBRs deliberately drew fire to locate the enemy's positions for the helicopters.

The first pass by the Hueys revealed ten Viet Cong groups on the bank. PBR 105 took one hit forward and one aft, with no serious

U.S. Marines are transported up the Saigon River in a U.S. Navy river patrol boat (PBR).

damage and no one was killed or wounded. The gunships were given a clear field of fire to destroy the VC positions but the patrol boats hit the junks, which were seven in number with machine-gun fire. One junk was badly damaged but it did not sink.

By now it was estimated that a whole battalion of Viet Cong had attempted to make the river crossing and their fleet included as many as 75 sampans. While the helicopters raked the bank many

One of many PBRs which patrolled the 3,000 miles of navigable waterways of the Mekong Delta.

Crewmen of the Vietnamese Junk Force search a fishing vessel for Viet Cong arms and ammunition.

VC were knee-deep in water attempting to get ashore. The PBRs were joined by two more two-boat patrols.

Petty Officer Williams had shown great initiative and skill in maneuvering his fighting patrol to await the helicopters and even greater courage in engaging the enemy whose superior numbers became increasingly apparent throughout the three hour action on October 31, 1966.

At one point of time, PBR 105 and 107 were confronted with two junks and eight sampans crammed with VC whose fire power was augmented by heavy automatic fire from ashore. Williams with utter disregard for his own safety exposed himself to the withering hail of enemy fire to direct counter fire and inspire the actions of his patrol.

When it was virtually dark, Williams ordered his patrol searchlight to be turned on to light up the area to identify targets; and at the same time revealing his own boats as targets. For his extraordinary heroism and exemplary fighting spirit in the face of great risks Boatswain's Mate First Class James E. Williams, United States Navy, was awarded the Congressional Medal of Honor.

No material of intelligence value was recovered from the sampans which could be reached by PBRs. Many sampans had drifted into brush and were inaccessible. Debris, clothing and seven large pools of blood were floating in the area of the battle. The PBRs and helicopters sunk or damaged most of the vessels in the VC fleet. An ammunition junk had been blown to bits.

Both PBR 105 and 107 had received superficial hits but continued with their patrol into the night. The incident off Ngo Hiep island that day had seen more action than most of the river patrols. Some missions went off without incident but the sailors who manned the PBRs knew that death lurked day and night on the waterways of the Mekong Delta.

The crew of a PBR man their weapons during a routine patrol as their boat moves in cautiously to the river bank.

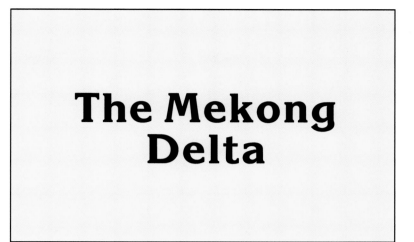

The Mekong Delta

Vietnam appears on a map of Asia as an elongated figure eight along the eastern edge of the Indochinese peninsula. It is made up of two river basins – the Red and the Mekong – separated by a narrow chain of mountains backing an even narrower coastal plain.

The Red River delta is separated from the coastal lowlands to the south by low lying hills that also serve as the boundary between the old provinces of Tonkin and Annam. Elsewhere the delta is surrounded by rugged mountains that jut abruptly out of the alluvial plain to form the frontier shared with China and Laos.

During the nineteenth century the French had used the waterways comprising the Red, Black and Clear Rivers in the north and the Mekong, Bassac, Dong Nai, Saigon and Van Co Rivers of Cochinchina in the south in the conquest of Indochina. Even in peacetime most of the traffic in the north of Vietnam was by waterways.

In wartime, with roads and railways frequently cut by enemy action, the French estimated that 90 per cent of traffic would be by inland waterway. It is not surprising therefore that in the First Indochina War (1946-54) the French should turn to the waterways of the north where the action was to take place for military operations.

When the French marched again into Hanoi in 1946, which was then the administrative capital of the whole of Indochina, Ho Chi Minh's nationalist forces were already well organized. In the riverine theater, the French started out with craft that were available locally – native or left by the Japanese – which they modified with armor and armament.

At the end of World War II Admiral Mountbatten's Southeast

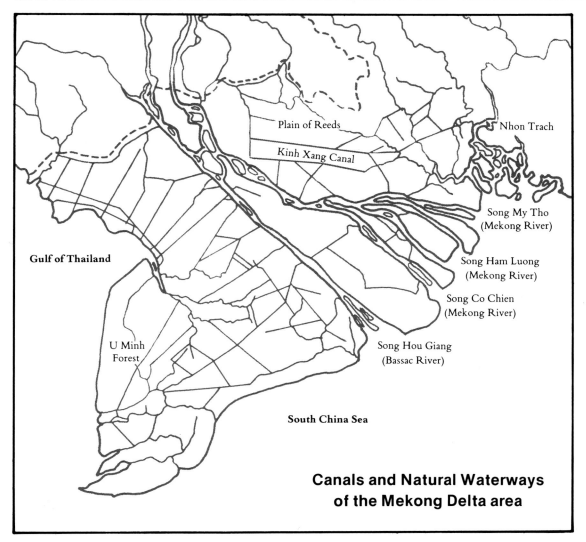

**Canals and Natural Waterways
of the Mekong Delta area**

The Mekong Delta.

Asia Command (SEAC) was centered on Saigon where the British received the surrender of the Japanese forces in Indochina. Before the war ended Mountbatten had been planning an amphibious invasion of Malaya and some of the landing craft assembled for the operation in 1946 were handed over to the French Navy.

Originally, the responsibility of the French Army, by 1946 the French Navy had organised river flotillas that were designed for the transport of 'Commandos' and river patrols. In 1947, the river flotillas were designated Divisions Navales D'Assaut (naval assault divisions abbreviated to *dinassauts*).

The divisions were organised initially to provide transport with support escort. In time their composition changed according to the areas of operation. Each flotilla had from 12 to 18 craft ranging from LCVPs (landing craft, vehicle or personnel) to LSSLs (landing ships, support, large) and contained at least these elements.

Command and fire support – 1 LCI (landing craft, infantry) or LSSL

Transport – 1 LCT (landing craft, tank)

Landing and support – 1 LCM (landing craft, medium and 4 LCVPs)

Patrol and liaison – 1 Harbor vessel.

The flotilla could transport and land an infantry force of about 700 men and their equipment. At first the flotillas were very successful in the role as raiders. However, when the Viet Minh massed their forces they proved less effective towards the end of the campaign. The *dinassauts* nevertheless reappeared again in similar form in the American Mobile Riverine Force (Task Force 117) of the Vietnam War.

South Vietnam, formerly Cochinchina had 3,200 miles of navigable waterways. The Mekong, which is one of the world's longest rivers rises in South Tsinghai Province in China and flows for 2,600 miles through Southeast Asia into the South China Sea.

The Mekong Delta extends from Saigon south and west to the Gulf of Thailand and the border with Cambodia. The Delta, its geography, and climate are described here in some detail, since this maze of waterways was to be the scene of a major conflict involving the U.S. and South Vietnamese navies against the Viet Cong.

With an area of about 24,800 square miles and an estimated eight million inhabitants, the Mekong Delta constitutes about one-fourth of the land area of South Vietnam. The Delta is generally a flat alluvial plain created by the Mekong River and tributaries. Most of the land surface is covered by rice paddies, making the area one of the world's most productive in rice growing.

The Delta had poor overland communications criss-crossed by a complex network of rivers, canals, streams and ditches and was subjected to extensive and prolonged flooding. There was only one major hard road surface, Route 4, which extended from Saigon south to Ca Mau, traversing the Delta and linking many of the larger towns.

The secondary roads were poorly surfaced and in the mid-1960s had deteriorated because of the lack of maintenance. Any movement by road was best during the dry season – November to March – when paddies were dry and would support light tracked vehicles and wheeled artillery.

> **Besides the Mekong and its tributaries, U.S. riverine forces had to control over 3000 miles of canals and waterways.**

Movement was poorest during the wet season – May to October, when paddies were flooded. It was restricted all year round by the network of rivers, canals, streams and ditches. There were many swamps, marshes and forests, generally bordering the sea coast.

One especially swampy area was termed in the Vietnam War, the Rung Sat Special Zone, the only territorial command of the South Vietnamese Navy. The name 'Rung Sat' means dense jungle and well describes the extensive mangrove swamp through which passed the main ship canal that linked Saigon with the sea.

The Viet Cong found the relative inaccessibility of the Rung Sat,

South Vietnamese fire an 81-mm mortar aboard a former French *commandament* river vessel.

its proximity to Saigon, and its position astride the III and IV Corps Tactical Zones combined to make it an excellent place to maintain a large base from which small parties of VC could emerge to strike terror on the waterways and in the villages.

In sharp contrast to the limited land transportation, the Delta had a highly developed inland waterway system. There is evidence that the inhabitants of the region discovered the means of improving natural drainage as long ago as 800 AD and succeeding generations have continued the work.

By the time the Vietnam War commenced in the mid-1960s the 1,500 miles of natural waterways were supplemented by almost twice the length of land-cut canals in varying depth, width and in good to poor condition.

The wet season in the Delta actually lasts from mid-May through early October, as the southwest monsoon drenches the lowlands with rain accumulated from its passage over thousands of miles of ocean. Unleashing a torrent of savage thunderstorms in May, the weather then lapses into a monotonous pattern of afternoon showers.

The rainfall and cloudiness reach a peak in July and August, when heavy downpours wash out the horizon and reduce visibility to zero. The fall transition period lasts barely a month, followed by the northeast monsoon season, which brings cool, dry weather from November until early March.

The wet season permits the deliberate flooding of the rice paddies, but also causes some unavoidable flooding as rivers overflow their banks. Waterways grow wider, sharply limiting cross-country traffic of military transport. Off road movement of troops and vehicles causes damage to crops and drainage systems, and would therefore be unpopular with the farmers.

One third of the Delta is marsh, forest or swamp forest. In the north lies the Plain of Reeds, a flat grassy basin. During the wet season it is generally inundated with water to a depth of six to nine feet; during the dry season much of the plain dries out with the reeds often standing ten feet tall. The reeds and grass often act like tinder when exposed to intense heat and fires frequently occur.

Apart from the monsoon floods, riverine operations in the Mekong Delta in the Vietnam War had to deal daily with the strong influence of sea tides along the inland waterways throughout the region. The twice daily tidal flows influence the velocity of current and have an important bearing on the feasibility of navigation on many waterways.

Enter the Brown Water Navy!

Despite massive U.S. aid, at least one third of South Vietnam was under Communist control by 1960.

Forces in the Delta

During 1965 when the creation of a U.S. riverine force for operations in the Mekong Delta was being discussed, there were three basic considerations that weighed heavily in favor of the force. Firstly, Americans have a tradition for river forces, stemming from the Civil War, particularly Union operations in the Mississippi basin.

Secondly American Naval and Marine Corps observers in the Indochina War had been very impressed by the *dinassauts*, in a period when the helicopter was still in its infancy and of poor roadways; the rivers were the most reliable routes through which units could be channeled to raid the Viet Minh lairs.

Thirdly, and most importantly, the situation in the Mekong Delta seemed rife for exploitation by river patrols and waterborne strike forces. The great strategic and economic importance of South Vietnam's extensive inland waterways made it clear that the Brown Water Navy would be to the fore. The Mekong Delta contained the largest segment of South Vietnam's population and constituted the country's 'bread basket'.

As elsewhere in Vietnam, the enemy by 1966 had both a political and military organization in the Delta. In mid-1966 the estimated strength of the Viet Cong in the IV Corps Tactical Zone, which corresponded roughly to the Delta was 82,545 men and women. Of these 19,290 were combat troops; 1,290 were support troops; 50,765 were local part-time guerrillas; and 11,220 were political agents.

It was known from the start that Viet Cong survival depended on support from the local population, captured equipment from Republic of Vietnam units, and supplies furnished by the People's

South Vietnamese Marines are embarked on a U.S. Navy inshore patrol craft (PCF) on the Con Mau River.

Democratic Republic of Vietnam – primarily weapons and ammunition – infiltrated by sea or by the Ho Chi Minh land route.

Base areas such as the Plain of Reeds, the U Minh Forest, and the Cam Zon Secret Zone west of My Tho served as sites for schools for military and political training and 'combat villages' were built, organized and controlled by the Viet Cong. Cambodia also provided a service area for main and local VC forces.

The Viet Cong forces in 1965 were as well armed as the North Vietnam regulars. The family of 7.62-mm weapons manufactured by the Chinese communists were first captured in the Delta on December 11, 1964 by ARVN troops. The capture included automatic rifles, carbines and light machine-guns all of Soviet design.

The Viet Cong operated in the Mekong Delta in much the same

A U.S. Navy man posted on a river boat test fires a 'Zippo' flame thrower against a river bank.

way as other battle zones. They lived in outposts in the jungle underbrush and in the villages where the VC could not be distinguished from the local inhabitants. Every day, the main water routes were choked with junks and sampans. Their cargoes often concealed weapons and supplies for the Viet Cong.

The VC usually made 'hit and run raids' involving only small numbers of men but they were also known to attack with several battalions. In January 1963 at At Bac, a Viet Cong force engaged a superior Vietnam Army force that assaulted their position with the heliborne forces in conjunction with conventional ground movement. Five helicopters were destroyed and nine damaged as the VC inflicted heavy casualties and withdrew.

In December 1964, two regiments of the Viet Cong 9th Division seized the Catholic village of Binh Gia. During the next four days the enemy ambushed and virtually destroyed the Vietnamese 33d

In this typical Mekong Delta scene, a PBR transits a river full of small civilian craft.

Ranger Battalion and 4th Marine Battalion and inflicted heavy casualties on an armored relief force.

There were two main divisions of waterborne offensive to eliminate the Viet Cong guerrillas from the Mekong Delta: River Patrol Force Operation 'Game Warden', controlled by the U.S. Navy's Task Force 116 and the Riverine Assault Force (Task Force 117), which was a combined Army and Navy effort.

The River Patrol Force first went into action on December 18, 1965. A curfew was imposed in the Delta prohibiting local river traffic after dark. The daily routine involved stopping and searching suspicious river craft for military cargoes. A number of local land units assisted the American Forces in the Delta.

In 1966 most of the Mekong Delta was included in the IV Corps Tactical Zone, although Gia Dinh Province, Long An Province, and the Rung Sat Special Zone in the north were part of III Corps Tactical Zone. The IV Corps Tactical Zone in turn was divided into three South Vietnamese divisional areas.

In the north the South Vietnamese 7th Division had its headquarters at My Tho; in the center was the 9th Division with its HQ at Sa Dec; and in the south was the 29th Division with its HQ at Bau Lieu. In 1966 the South Vietnamese Army's assigned strength in IV Corps Zone averaged 40,000 men. In addition to the three divisions, there were five Ranger battalions and three armored squadrons.

South Vietnam paramilitary forces included Regional Forces, Popular Forces, Civilian Irregular Defense Group (CIDG) troops – who were the Montagnard tribesmen lead by the U.S. Special Forces A-Teams – and the National Police. After the devastating VC attacks on CIDG camps in the early years, friendly Chinese mercenaries called Nungs were recruited to strengthen the force.

In 1966, Regional and Popular Forces manned outposts and watchtowers scattered throughout the Delta. Poorly supported and highly vulnerable to VC attack, both these forces had high desertion rates. The CIDG troops and their Green Beret sponsors were employed generally (in the Delta region) along the Cambodian border, as part of the effort to seal the frontier against the VC and NVA.

The National Police were organized as a paramilitary force along the lines of the French *gendarmerie*, and performed similar functions. One of these in the Vietnam case was to arrest the hated tax collectors who forcibly extorted protection money from the Delta farmers. If the farmers did not pay their 'taxes', which funded the Viet Cong, their homes and property would be destroyed.

> **Ammunition came cheap: 100,000 rounds were fired for every soldier killed by U.S. forces in Vietnam.**

A PCF of the U.S. Navy patrols the Rack-Gia Ha Tien Canal in a search for Viet Cong hide-outs.

It was against this background that the basic decisions for the creation of an American riverine force were made in 1965 and 1966. The U.S. Navy reacted to the challenge swiftly. Searches were made for old World War II landing craft which appeared in new forms on drawing boards. The Navy was about to write a new and fascinating chapter in its history.

'Game Warden'

From December 1965 to March 1966, the U.S. Navy was busy procuring river patrol boats (PBR) in the United States. Crews, who were given training in weapons handling and jungle survival, learned the ropes at the Coronado and Marine Island bases, California. The river division (PBR) which deployed in Vietnam was a total of two 10-boat sections which operated from bases along the major rivers or from ships afloat in the rivers.

The PBR, the workhorse of the River Patrol Force, was manned by a crew of four sailors, and was equipped with surface radar and two radios. The boats were armed with a twin-mount .50-caliber machine-gun forward, a .30-caliber machine-gun aft, and a rapid fire .40-mm grenade launcher.

The first version of the boat, the Mark I, performed well in river patrol operations but was plagued with continual fouling of the water-jet engines by weeds and floating detritus. In addition, the fiberglass hull of the boats was often damaged when Vietnamese sampans came alongside for inspection.

The PBR design was adapted from a commercial fiberglass-hull plastic boat especially suited for shallow-water operations with trainable water jet nozzles in lieu of conventional propeller or rudder. The Mark IIs, first in action in the Delta in December 1966, brought with them improved jet pumps which reduced fouling.

The Mark II was slightly larger all round than the Mark I. Its displacement was 8 tons: length 32 feet: beam 11.5 feet: draft 2.2 feet. Its three .50-caliber machine-guns were placed twin mounted forward, single aft. It was also armed with a 40-mm grenade launcher. The Mark II's main engines were two geared diesels; water jets were fitted. It had a speed of 29 knots and a complement of four or five enlisted men.

The afloat bases or 'mother' ships, were either World War II dock landing ships or tank landing ships. It is difficult to imagine rather crudely designed amphibious vessels could be converted to provide all the base facilities required by the PBR crews but these old ships succeeded in doing their job.

The afloat fleet consisted at various times of *Tortuga* (LSD 26), *Belle Grove* (LSD 26), *Cornstock* (LSD 19), *Floyd County* (LSD 762), and *Jennings County* (LST 821), *Garrett County* (LST 786) and *Hunterden County* (LST 838) during 1967 and 1968. Each floating base was equipped with a helicopter.

U.S. Marines are carried up the Saigon River in a PBR during Operation 'Big Muddy', January 1969.

A key component of the 'Game Warden' operation was its air support element. Initially, the Army deployed detachments of two UH-1B Iroquois helicopters and their crews to the PBR bases on land and afloat. Beginning in August 1966, however, air crews of the Navy's Helicopter Support Squadron 1 replaced the Army personnel.

Then on April 1, 1967, the Navy activated Helicopter Attack (light) Squadron (HAL) 3 at Vung Tau to assume the overall responsibility for providing Task Force 116 with aerial fire support, observation and medical evacuation. By September 1968, the 421-man 'Seawolves' Squadron controlled detachments of two helicopters each at five shore stations, and on board three LSTs.

The watchful eyes of the PBR crews were trained by day and night for the slightest sign of enemy activity.

The minesweeper played a vital role in Task Force 116. Clearing the rivers of mines was nowhere more crucial than in the region near Saigon, the country's most important port. Viet Cong mining of the main shipping channel, the Long Tau River, which wound its way through the Rung Sat Special Zone south of the capital could have had a devastating effect on the allied war effort.

Consequently, on May 20, 1966, the Navy established Mine Squadron II at Nha Be under Commander Task Force 116. From then until 1968, 12 or 13 minesweeping boats (MSB) reactivated in the United States were in constant service. In July 1967, the minesweeping force was increased with the arrival at Nha Be of six landing craft (LCM(M)) specially configured to sweep mines.

The 'Game Warden' mission was to deny the enemy use of the major waterways and it was a constant responsibility from the day Task Force 116 was created – December 18, 1965 – until the day in 1973 when the U.S. pulled out of the country. A section of ten PBRs operated with the responsibility for 30 miles of waterway.

Patrols were normally conducted by two-boat teams operating within radar range of one another for mutual support. Within each boat section, one team patrolled during daylight hours and three teams patrolled at night. The fifth team remained at base to service the boats. Patrols normally extended over 12 hours.

The initial 'Game Warden' organization included a Delta River Patrol Group and a Rung Sat Special Zone Patrol Group. Of these two areas, the Rung Sat was considered the most important because of its access to the port of Saigon.

At the end of 1965, four Saigon-based landing craft with American crews had already been deployed to augment the South Vietnamese Navy's surveillance of the Rung Sat. Shortly afterwards Swift boats borrowed from coastal patrol operations were used in the Rung Sat, and in March 1966 four minesweepers were sent to the area.

That same month, the new Hatteras hull, 31-foot PBR Mark II began arriving in Vietnam and were sent to relieve the coastal vessels in the Rung Sat so they were able to return to their 'Market Time' assignments. 'Market Time' was the code name for the U.S.

More U.S. servicemen were sent to Vietnam than to the Western Front in World War I or to Korea.

A boatswain's mate mans his machine gun mounted on a PCF during a patrol off the Ca Mau Peninsula.

Navy's commitment to patrolling the coast to intercept vessels, usually coastal junks conveying supplies to the VC from the north.

As if to underscore the importance the Americans attached to the Rung Sat, the Viet Cong badly damaged a Panamanian freighter crossing the zone in February 1966. A few days later, a Vietnamese fuel barge was fired on and commercial shipping, already uneasy

A bluejacket aboard a PBR fires a flaming arrow at a bamboo hut concealing a fortified VC bunker.

11% of U.S. battle-deaths in Vietnam were caused by Communist booby-traps.

over the surprises awaiting them in the Rung Sat's mangroves, became increasingly apprehensive.

The Navy was asked by Gen. Westmoreland to use its Amphibious Ready Group/Special Landing Force (ARG/SLF) to clear the area. This was agreed upon and on March 14, a reinforced U.S. Marine battalion landed in the Rung Sat for operations that lasted three weeks. In the later stages of this operation code-named Operation 'Jackstay', two battalions of Vietnamese Marines joined in the sweep.

In one month, August 1966, Viet Cong mines in the Long Tau River heavily damaged SS *Baton Rouge Victory*, a Vietnamese motor launch minesweeper, and minesweeper MSB 54. In November, MSB 54 again was mined, and this time sunk and on the last day of the year American forces for the first time discovered a Soviet-made contact mine in the shipping channel.

Minesweeping operations by the U.S. and Vietnamese units were intensified as a result, but the enemy continued to focus on the anti-mining effort. In February 1967, Communist recoilless rifle fire and mines heavily damaged MSB 49, destroyed MSB 45, and inflicted lesser damage on other 'Game Warden' vessels.

By the spring of 1967, the rapid build-up of allied forces in the Rung Sat area, the refinement of tactics and improvement of weapons systems began to reduce the enemy effectiveness. During the year Vietnamese Regional Forces and the U.S. Army 9th Infantry Division troops fought aggressive actions ashore in coordination with the helicopter, PBR and MSB units.

The River Patrol Force commander led other naval forces as well, including the Navy's own commandos, the 'Sea-Air-Land' SEALs. In mid-1968, the 211-man SEAL Team 1 fielded 12, 14-man platoons, each composed of two squads. Generally four or five of the platoons were deployed to South Vietnam where at least three were in action in the Rung Sat Special Zone.

Beginning in early 1967, the Atlantic Fleet's SEAL TEAM 2 provided another three platoons, two of which were stationed with the 'Game Warden' units at Can Tho. These units started SEAL operations in the central Delta area. Although focused primarily on the areas to the south and west of Saigon, SEAL operations were also mounted in the I and II Corps Tactical Zones.

These elite naval units carried out day and night ambushes, hit and run raids, reconnaissance patrols, salvage dives, and special intelligence operations. Normally operating in six-man squads, the SEALs used landing craft, SEAL team assault boats (STAB), 26-foot armored trimarans, PBRs, sampans and helicopters for trans-

portation to their objectives.

In the two boat, random boat patrols, the Task Force 116 sailors checked the cargo and identity papers of junks and sampans and sailing the waterways set up night ambushes at suspected enemy crossing points, provided transport for the SEALs and gunfire support, and enforced curfew restrictions in their sector, usually no more than 30 nautical miles from base.

The afloat base concept introduced by the Americans was a significant advance of the fixed base system used by the French. However, a further refinement to the shore basing concept was introduced in time with the construction of non-self-propelled floating bases (LSDs). Five of these were eventually used by 'Game Warden' and proved successful.

South Vietnamese sailing in a junk on the Perfume River have been stopped for questioning by a PBR crew.

Chasing Charlie

In mid-afternoon on October 26, 1966, PBRs 34 and 40, on normal patrol 42 miles downstream from Can Tho on the Bassac River, sighted three armed men in a sampan emerging from a stream on the southwest bank of the river, in an area known to be heavily invested with Viet Cong.

The patrol gave chase and fired two warning shots at the enemy before opening fire with 70 rounds of .50-caliber which set fire to the sampan. The boat reached a beach and its occupants took cover in the tree line. One M-79 round was fired into the area.

A Vietnamese National Policeman embarked in one of the PBRs directed a civilian sampan to attempt to recover the Viet Cong craft, but heavy fire broke out from the shore and the salvage efforts were abandoned. The patrol raked the brush along the river bank with machine-gun fire and quickly suppressed fire in turn coming from the area near the beached sampan.

When the shooting ceased from that area the enemy opened fire from further downstream with a .30-caliber machine-gun. The forward gunner in PBR 40, Radioman Second Class Terrance Jay Freund was hit in the chest by the first burst and knocked to the deck. He struggled to his feet, told the patrol officer he was 'okay' and returned firing, then slumped again.

Once again the Petty Officer returned to his post and continued to fire at the Viet Cong positions. He fell to the deck for a third and final time. Petty Officer Freund had fired over 200 rounds of .50 bullets at the enemy between the time he was hit and the time he died.

At 1630 hours, a 'Game Warden' helo fire team arrived on the scene and began to take the enemy under fire. Ten minutes later

PBRs 37 and 38 arrived in the area and were taken under fire by rockets and grenades from the beach. U.S. Army helicopters now joined in the battle, followed by a South Vietnamese river assault group (RAG).

The combined forces made firing runs over the beach for 40 minutes when they cleared the area for a U.S. Air Force F-100 Supre Sabre strike, which was later cancelled. Around 1800 hours, the Army helicopters, freshly rearmed delivered more fire at the ambush positions. The Navy helicopters also returned to the area after rearming and carried on the attack.

The River Assault Group 25, supported by the PBRs entered a canal in the area and set up a blocking force behind the ambush. At 1900 hours, a RAG monitor entered the stream with smaller river craft and delivered 40-mm. fire. Shortly after the monitor strafed

A strike assault boat (STAB) makes a high speed river patrol close to the Cambodian border.

the area the Viet Cong broke contact and disappeared into the brush.

Thus another entry was made for the PBRs' records. The engagement had claimed one American life. There were four confirmed Viet Cong killed, one sampan burned and an estimated battalion size river crossing thwarted by the combined efforts of the U.S. and Vietnamese Navy units and Army and Navy aircraft.

On March 6, 1967, PBR 124 was on patrol on the Mekong River in the early hours of the morning when Seaman David G. Ouellet observed suspicious activity near the river bank. Seaman Ouellet shouted to his boat captain, and the boat turned to investigate.

While the PBR was making a high-speed run along the river bank, the young seaman spotted an incoming grenade falling toward the boat. He immediately left the protected position of his gun mount and ran aft the full length of the speeding boat,

Another strike boat (STAB) patrols a waterway near the Cambodian border at very high speed.

shouting to his fellow crew members to take cover.

Seeing the boat captain standing unprotected on the boat, Seaman Ouellet bounded onto the engine compartment cover, and pushed the captain down to safety. In the split second that followed the grenade's landing, and in the face of certain death, he fearlessly threw himself between the deadly missile and his shipmates.

Seaman David Ouellet, who was posthumously awarded the Congressional Medal of Honor for his extraordinary heroism took the full blast of the grenade fragments with his own body to protect his shipmates from injury and death.

SEAL operations, which were often brief encounters between the Navy commandos and VC acting singly or in pairs when a VC was killed or captured and his AK-47 and bag of rice impounded, built up to harassment of the Viet Cong in the Delta on a significant scale.

One of the many SEAL actions took place on March 2, 1969

U.S. Marines leave a landing craft on a sweep and clear mission after crossing a river near Danang.

when a squad of the Navy commandos were on an operation ten miles northeast of Vinh Long. A Vietnamese member of the team was dressed as a Viet Cong with an AK-47. The Vietnamese, who was a South Vietnamese Special Forces (LDNN) man questioned an old woman as to the whereabouts of the enemy.

The squad then patrolled to a nearby house and spotted two unarmed VC outside the house. As the SEALs approached the VC alerted those inside the building. The house was taken under fire. Seven VC ran out of the front door and one went out the back in an effort to escape. As a result seven VC were killed and one wounded.

The house was surrounded and Viet Cong who were sighted crouching in a bunker were urged to surrender. This failing, a SEAL threw a hand grenade into the bunker killing all three of its occupants. Three enemy sampans were destroyed and a complete B-40 rocket system as well as several personnel weapons were captured.

On October 31, 1972 Petty Officer Michael E. Thornton, an assistant U.S. Navy advisor, along with a U.S. Navy lieutenant

A UN-1D Huey helicopter used for medical evacuation is seen on the helopad of an armored troop carrier (ATC).

A U.S. Navy 'Sea-Air-Land' (SEAL) commando team watch for movement in a thick wooded area.

serving as senior advisor accompanied a three-man Vietnamese Navy SEAL patrol on an intelligence gathering mission against an enemy occupied naval river base.

Mounted in a PBR, the SEAL team went ashore close to their objective when suddenly they came under heavy fire. The patrol called in naval gunfire and then engaged the enemy in a fierce firefight, accounting for many casualties before moving back to the waterline to prevent encirclement.

The senior U.S. advisor was hit and at first believed to be dead. In spite of heavy fire, Petty Officer Thornton carried the lieutenant, who was seriously wounded and unconscious, to the water's edge. Thornton then inflated the officer's life jacket and began to swim towing the wounded man.

The two men were in the water for two hours before they were picked up by a patrol craft. Engineman Second Class Michael E. Thornton, USN, who was awarded the Congressional Medal of Honor for his bravery, was directly responsible for saving the life of his superior officer, and helping the SEALs to withdraw safely.

The Plain of Reeds

The Mekong Delta, south of Saigon, as we have learned was a vast flatland of winding rivers and interconnecting canals, mixed with rice paddies, bogs, trackless marsh and forest. Larger rivers featured floating rice, with stems 12 feet long. Paddy land, flooded enough to boast two rice plantings a year, was broken in places by waste areas of sedge marsh and palm swamp.

The lower regions were typically broken by sluggish tidal streams and channels fringed with dense mangrove and bottomless mud flats. With the exception of the Seven Mountains area along the western Cambodian border, the level plain was broken only by stream and canal banks, paddy dikes, and raised road beds.

Vast areas of the Mekong Delta were inundated by the rainy season and remained waterlogged for months. Dense forest swamps, such as the Nam Can forest on Ca Mau peninsula, also existed. Extensive and poorly drained, the marshy plains grew reeds that dwarfed the average man!

The U.S. Navy and the South Vietnamese Navy patrolled the navigable waterways but the U.S. Army was assigned the task of handling waterborne operations during the monsoon on the flooded rice marshes and lower Mekong Delta region. The Plain of Reeds had for centuries been a haven for guerrilla fighters. The Army force assigned to the area were the elite U.S. Special Forces, the Green Berets.

The Green Berets, who operated in the lower Delta region were mainly the B-Teams, although some of the 'Cidgees' (CIDG) tribesmen led by the A-Teams also served in the area. The camps in the monsoon virtually became floating bases. Until the combat airboats were introduced the Green Beret Navy used a collection of

The gunner in the U.S. Navy hovercraft operating in the Mekong Delta mans a .50 caliber machine gun.

sampans and small engine assault boats with outboard motors.

The Navy also sent PBRs and other small riverine craft. Even with conventional boats, Special Forces mobility was limited. Meadows of sea grass were dense enough to cause prop-fouling at low tide. Mangrove swamps blocked boat movement with 60-foot trees and mazes of gnarled roots formed slippery ledges surrounded by quick sand and soft, deep mud.

The freshwater swamps were filled with towering cajaput trees, which formed an unbroken jungle canopy. Small streams and canals hampered off-road movement. Many of the narrow, shallow waterways could be travelled only by sampans. Although rice-field dikes were generally low, tiny clusters of houses and Nypa palms, provided good opportunities for ambush.

The deep ditches around vegetable gardens offered excellent trenches and escape routes. Grassy marshes could be set ablaze in the dry season, creating confusion and smokescreens. The primitive watercraft initially available to the Green Berets afforded a flimsy method of transportation easily subject to ambush.

The Special Forces acquired a modified version of the 'swamp' buggy then popular with tourists in the Florida Everglades for combat patrols on the Plain of Reeds. The Hurricane Company's airboat was powered by a 180-hp Lycoming aircraft engine; it was 17 feet long and weighed 1,150 pounds.

An airboat of a Special Forces B-team leaves its docking facilities for a sortie on the Plain of Reeds.

Named the Aircat the airboat was capable of a speed of 38 mph while carrying a 300-lb load. They could skim over the aquatic grasses and leap rice-paddy dikes, requiring only a thumb's depth of water under their fiberglass and Styrofoam hulls. The use of airboats in combat was a relatively new development, but their versatility soon included patrolling, blocking escape avenues, reconnoitering, transporting reserves or supplies and providing medical evacuation.

Elaborate tactics were developed for racing over water and marsh in pairs or in massed formation to raid enemy strongpoints. Even ambush seemed feasible if the crews let the boats drift or if they silently paddled into position, opened fire with their machine- guns and then turned on their engines and sped off in pursuit.

The first two trained Special Forces airboat platoons arrived at Moc Hoa under Detachment B-41's responsibility on October 27, 1966. Altogether 54 Aircats were allocated to nine Delta stations. Advanced and unit training were completed at Moc Hoa and Cai Cai. The actual combat employment of airboats, however, had had to be learned by the Green Berets on a trial and error basis.

By mid-November 1966 the floodwaters had receded to a point that still precluded foot operations but made assault boat travel impossible. Airboats and Navy Patrol Air Cushion Vehicles (PAVC) dominated the Delta during this period, which lasted until December 12th.

Three giant U.S. Navy air cushion craft and 18 sailors were quartered at Moc Hoa during the last week of November and the first week of December. On November 21, the first of ten combined Navy PACV-Special Forces operations throughout Kien Tuong Province was launched. The PACV craft moved over both dry and flooded terrain, restricted only by tree lines, and high reeds that caused them to stall.

The highly effective, agile strike craft ranged across the countryside. One of the most successful actions occurred on November 2, 1966, when Detachment A-414 engaged a full company of Viet Cong irregulars. The PACV and airboat teams were called into the battle. They routed the VC, who attempted to flee into Cambodia.

This movement was quickly blocked by six helicopters that landed a mobile strike force (CIDG) company to seal off any escape. All forces converged on the trapped unit. After a fierce two-hour struggle, the entire VC company was annihilated, and only one CIDG soldier was wounded in exchange. Fifty sampans were destroyed, and an outboard motor lost in a previous battle recovered.

> **More Americans died in the 3 days of the Battle of Gettysburg than died in the first 2 years of U.S. deployment in Indochina.**

A suspected Viet Cong guerilla is taken into custody by the U.S. Navy crewmen of a PACV.

River Offensive

If the Ironclads of the Civil War and the more recent French *dinassauts* loomed in the minds of Gen. Westmoreland and his staff when planning combat objectives in the IV Corps Tactical Zone for 1965-66, it was the shortage of land suitable for bases that made the idea of floating barracks ships an urgent situation.

Throughout the Vietnam War, MACV was constantly frustrated by the South Vietnam government when making proposals for the deployment of American forces. In the Mekong Delta, which occupied almost the whole of IV Corps Tactical Zone, there was already a strong presence of ARVN troops and the huge civilian population lived in overcrowded conditions.

The South Vietnamese believed their army, which included a large paramilitary force was better able to deal with the Viet Cong than the Americans but as the American advisors had found, the South Vietnamese forces had their own political differences and were not always reliable in battle.

Clearly more punch was needed in the Delta, which was about to emerge as a major battle zone, than Task Force 116 and loyal Government troops could provide. An American riverine assault planning group went to Saigon to work with MACV. The battle manifesto that emerged called for the cooperation of the U.S. Navy and Army to produce a force based on the French experience, but one with greater capabilities.

World War II veterans remembered the huge tank landing ships (LST) had also been used as barracks ships to billet troops of the amphibious task forces and their equipment. In June 1966, two barracks ships were de-mothballed from an obscure corner of an

A U.S. Navy ATC provides cover while a Huey helicopter arrives to pick up casualties on the river bank.

The self propelled barracks ship USS *Benewah* lies in the Soi Ray River with her assault boats alongside.

Atlantic yard and towed to the Philadelphia yard for conversion.

Supply people of the U.S. Navy studied photographs of the French naval craft with their improvised and rather bizarre armor plating and hunted for LCM-6s, or LCM-8s (if they were available), which were the landing craft, medium, also of World War II vintage. Officials figured out how to get the LCMs to half-a-dozen shipyards that were contracted for the naval program.

Soon hammers were banging away and planners were grinding pencils shaping the new flotilla, which was called River Assault Flotilla One. An old repair ship, the USS *Askari*, a veteran of Vietnam in 1954, was re-commissioned for a second trip to

Indochina.

The Philadelphia Naval Yard was dry-dock deep with problems on the two barracks ships, the *Benewah* (APB 35) and the *Colleton* (APB 36). Washington DC was struggling to find and then position new equipment for the force. Shipyards from Key West, Florida, to Seattle, Washington, labored on changing the classic LCMs into something their original designers would have never believed possible.

Task Force 117, as the mobile riverine force was designated by the U.S. Navy, consisted of a small fleet of mini monsters crewed by blue jackets and equipped to support assault troops of the 9th

Over half of the South Vietnamese population inhabited the Mekong Delta.

U.S. Infantry Division. All naval personnel and the Army brigade on active duty were embarked in the self-propelled barracks ships.

TF 117's combat craft, which were heavily armored and armed, consisted of a monitor (MON), which aptly used the classic name for a river gunboat; an assault support patrol boat (ASPB); a command and control boat (CCB); armored troop carriers (ATC), which were at the heart of the matter; and various converted minesweepers.

At Vallejo, California, the U.S. Navy set up a training center for the boat crews. The sailors were taught the basics of riverine warfare. Instruction was given in swimming, first aid, day and night navigation and those endless hours in the rivers and sloughs around Vallejo gave the blue jackets the start they needed. The crews also received survival and escape and evasion simulated experience at Warner Springs, California.

The 9th Infantry Division was activated at Fort Riley, Kansas. The division was organized as a standard infantry division of the U.S. Army. The formation was composed of nine infantry battalions of which one was initially mechanized (a U.S. battalion numbers approximately 700 men). The division had a cavalry squadron and the normal artillery and other supporting units.

As 1966 progressed Gen. Westmoreland became increasingly anxious to use the 9th Division in the Mekong Delta. Overcoming objections from South Vietnamese commanders, Westmoreland chose a Delta land base for the division near My Tho. The proposed location of the base did not appear as a name on the map so the general called the site Dong Tam, which in Vietnamese means literally 'united hearts and minds'.

An idea born in 1966 was to become an early 1967 reality. At the turn of the year the *Askari* (ARL 30), the *Henrico* (APB 45) and the *Westfield County* (LST 1169) were on their way to Southeast Asia with the first of the converted LCMs on board.

And two months after her departure on February 22, the *Benewah* (APB 35), RIVERFLOTONE's huge ugly green flagship pushed over the horizon into Vung Tau harbor. The *Colleton* (APB 36) joined the growing naval force in Vietnam and in May the leading elements of the riverine assault force moved to Dong Tam.

By this time, the 2d Brigade, 9th Infantry Division was in country and blooded in action in the Rung Sat Special Zone. As fully organized, the Mobile Riverine Force consisted of the 2d Brigade, augmented in mid-1968 by the 3d Brigade, and the Navy element. The stage was set for chasing Charlie by amphibious maneuver on the Mekong waterways.

> **Saigon relied on the Mekong Delta for two-thirds of its essential rice supplies.**

Task Force 117

A high velocity jet system installed on an ATC fires a water stream at an enemy bunker.

In mounting a riverine assault operation, there were a number of factors to be taken into consideration. The brigade commander or a higher echelon Army commander at MACV usually selected the area of operations and the targets. The planning staff using the commander's directives and guidance began by outlining the scheme of maneuver in the objective area.

From the attack, the plan unfurled backwards, covering in turn

the landing or assault, movement by water to the objective, and the loading and embarking phases. Special considerations included the suitability of waterway routes into the area of operations; whether the river banks made good landing sites, and mooring for barge-mounted artillery.

The operational order which embodied such information included intelligence on the enemy's situation, naval and aerial fire support and weather forecast. A map of the waterways to be used furnished tides, widths and depth of streams, obstacles of various types, bridges, shoals, and mud banks and other navigation data.

No two assault riverine operations were the same. Over the first and crucial year a general pattern was developed but there were as many variations as there were to be missions. The pattern actually began the day before the scheduled operation, when the sailor crews loaded their boats with water, fuel, ammunition and C-rations. The boats were checked from top to bottom for things that might cause trouble the following day.

That evening the boat captains assembled on board the flagship *Benewah* for the Division commander's briefing. The essential orders were then distributed – movement plans, check points, signal schedules, codes and intelligence reports were noted. The captains groping their way in the dark made their way back to their boats to pass the word to the crews. The night watch was set and the rest of the men grabbed a few hours' sleep.

Early in the morning, often very early in the morning, the exact time being determined by the distance to the landing zone, all the boats cleared the pontoons where they were moored alongside their barracks ships and formed up into a circle. Three troop carriers then returned to pick up a company of soldiers, who had also received their orders the previous evening.

A reserve ATC stood by in case of trouble. Once the company was on board the boats cast off and rejoined the circle. The procedure was repeated until all the troops needed for the operation were in their boats and ready to move off. The monitors and command and communication boats came alongside to pick up command personnel.

On the signal, two minesweepers headed out into the night and the circling boats pulled off into a long, silent, fearsome column behind them. The troops aboard the ATCs lost little time in draping themselves over the steel decks, ammo boxes and each other to read or sleep until the boats turned off the rivers to head down the smaller streams.

The minesweepers leading the column were normally the ASPBs,

An assault support patrol boat (ASPB) moves alongside an ATC in a sweep for VC command detonated mines.

which also provided fire support. Rifle companies were usually embarked in a River Assault Section consisting of one monitor and three troop carriers. Boats within a section maintained intervals of about 20 yards moving in column; sections 150 to 200 yards.

Here the sweeps were ordered to stream their gear: general quarters was signalled and the sailors took refuge in their flak jackets, steel helmets and gun mounts. As the boats moved into the small stream leading to their objective, a helicopter overhead surveyed the situation. The fire support boats opened up to make the Viet Cong keep their heads down.

Sometimes the Air Force bombed the landing zones. Other times Army artillery pounded the area. Not infrequently a combination of the two were used. Shortly after dawn the boats reached the landing zones where on signal they turned in groups and ran their bows up to the stream banks with the lead minesweepers and monitors moved into position to cover the landing.

The safety hooks came off and the ramps went down. The troops moved out with their weapons poised for action. The landing may have taken place in mangrove swamp, rice paddy or Nipa palm thicket but the troops knew only too well that whatever the cover, the same miserable Delta mud would be under it.

The boats then backed off and established blocking patrols; some beached and watched and waited. While the troops were ashore sampans were stopped and searched, men whose identification papers were not in order were detained for questioning by Vietnamese police officials and war.supplies confiscated.

When the troops called for fire support from the riverine force the boats moved in and opened up with their heavier weapons; sometimes more supplies were needed ashore; or the wounded needed urgent evacuation; often the troops had to be moved swiftly to another location.

Some boats were assigned special missions. A medical aid station, which carried doctors, medics, medical supplies and a built in helo-pad went up stream to pick up casualties. An ATC acted as a refueler and another fitted with a helo-pad was ready to refuel helicopters.

Marines assigned to these missions travelling in ATCs specialized in gathering information on water depths, currents and tides in the uncharted streams. An Explosive Ordnance Disposal (EOD) Team was also embarked in an ATC and ready to blow up anything that might impede progress or help the enemy.

After two or three days when the infantry had finished their sweep, or when the battle was over if they had encountered the enemy in force, the boats closed in to pick them up. At the sight of an identifying smoke signal the boats moved into the banks, lowered the ramps and the wet, muddy, exhausted soldiers emerged from the bushes and clambered on board.

The trip back to the MRB was altogether a happier one than the inward journey. War stories grew in dimension as they were retold throughout the boats. Talk was about wives, girlfriends and cars. It was mostly happy talk as all concerned were happy to be alive and heading back to the safety and comfort of the mobile river base.

Tomorrow, or the next day, the boat crews would check their boats, load them with C-rations, water, fuel and ammunition, the boat captains would be on their way to the evening briefing. . . .

> **By the time U.S. forces moved into the war, the Communists had infiltrated some 50,000 of their men into the South.**

The Riverine Fleet

Altogether eight World War II barracks ships were de-mothballed at the time of the Vietnam War but only the *Benewah* (APB 35), *Colleton* (APB 36), *Mercer* (APB 39) and the *Nueces* (APB 40) went into active service in Southeast Asia. The *Benewah* and *Colleton* were recommissioned on January 28, 1967 and the *Mercer* and *Nueces* in 1968 but *Colleton* was decommissioned in 1968.

The displacement of the ex-LST type APBs was 2,189 (light) tons; 4,080 full load: length 328 feet: beam 50 feet: draft 11 feet: main engines – diesels (General Motors); 1,600 to 1,800 bhp: two shafts: speed 10 knots. The barracks ship was armed with two 3-inch guns (single); eight 40-mm guns (two quad mounts); ten .30- and eight .50-caliber machine-guns.

The complement of the barracks ship was 12 officers and 186 enlisted men and the billeting capacity 900 men, which represented the 2d Brigade battalion on active rosta and the naval crews who handled the riverine assault boats. For the troops and boat crews the barracks ships represented the 'Hiltons' of base facilities in an operational war zone.

The living and most working places were air-conditioned. Messing facilities were sumptuous as compared with facilities in the field. Facilities included rest rooms, cinema, chapel, laundry, library and tailor shop.

Evaporators produced up to 40,000 gallons of fresh water every day. A 16-bed hospital with X-Ray room, a dental room and pharmacy were provided and there was in addition a bacteriological laboratory for analytical research.

The Mobile Riverine Force units rotated between the afloat base and Dong Tam, the main Delta base near My Tho. At this location

the Army's engineers and the Navy's Seabees had built a complex especially for the joint riverine operations. The base contained barracks, mess halls, repair shops, floating crane, C-130 airstrip, small drydocks and waterfront facilities for the river craft.

Another batch of ex-LSTs were used for supplies and could carry troops. These included *Vernon County* (LST 1168), *Whitfield County* (LST 1169), *Washtenshaw County* (LST 1166). *Windham County* (LST 1170), *Caroline County* (LST 525), *Kemper County* (LST 854) and *Sedgwick County* (LST 1123).

The support squadron was further supplemented by *Askari* (APL 30), *Satyr* (ARL 23), *Indra* (ARL 37), APL 26, YRBM 17, YTB 84, YTB 85 and *Cohoes* (AN 78). The repair ship *Askari* had a 'can do' anything reputation and was usually as good as its word.

The Monitor (MON), a converted LCM-6, was heavily armored

with bar and plate armor and armed with a variety of weapons. These craft provided the fire support for the flotilla as well as security for the afloat bases.

The vessel, which was 60 feet in length, displaced 80 tons. It was powered by two diesels and made eight knots. The guns were one 105-mm howitzer or 81-mm mortar; two 20-mm and three .30-caliber machine-guns; and two 40-mm high velocity grenade launchers.

The howitzer or mortar was replaced on some of the monitors by two Army M10-8 flame throwers. These craft were referred to as 'Zippos' (a popular type of cigarette lighter) and the monitor the 'battleship' of the riverine fleet.

Similarly converted from LCM-6s, the Command and Control Boat (CCB) served as an afloat command post providing command

A Monitor (MON) uses its flame thrower to destroy an enemy ambush position along a narrow river.

and communication facilities for the assault force and boat group commanders. These armored craft carried two 20-mm guns and two .30-caliber machine-guns and two 40-mm high velocity grenade launchers.

The Armored Troop Carrier (ATC), another of the LCM-6s breed, carried the assault infantry of the riverine flotilla. These craft could also carry small vehicles, artillery and supplies. Some of the ATCs were fitted with light steel helicopter platforms to facilitate the evacuation of wounded men.

A winch fitted to the fantail for chain drag equipment was used to sweep for command detonated mines. A modified ATC served as a refueler for the river fleet. The complement was 7 crew and troop capacity 40 fully armed infantry.

The ATC was armed with two 20-mm guns; two to six .30- and two .50-caliber machine-guns; one 40-mm high velocity grenade launcher; and two 40-mm low velocity grenade launchers.

The Assault Support Patrol Boat (ASPB), again a converted LCM-6 served as an escort for other river craft, and also provided mine counter-measures during river operations. Hulls were steel welded and the heavy scale of armament varied.

The ASPB, which was developed by the Sikorsky Aircraft Division of United Aircraft Corporation, was 50 feet in length and the beam 17 feet. The craft was powered by three gas turbines, driving three water jets. The speed of 40 knots demonstrated the potential movement of the ASPB in the close support role.

The craft had a lightweight 105-mm howitzer gun and two 20-mm cannon mounted in a tank-like turret with a 360 degree field of fire. A smaller forward mount was remote controlled and initially contained two 7.62-mm machine-guns and a 40-mm grenade launcher, but the machine-guns were later replaced with two 20-mm cannons.

Also fitted for minesweeping, a radar tripod mast was placed aft. The Stewart Seacraft, another brand of ASPB, was similar to the Sikorsky model but an 81-mm mortar replaced the howitzer. Both craft, heavily armored, were designed so that the main turret and engines were on shock springs to reduce the effects of mine explosions.

The ASPB, in addition to the howitzer or mortar, carried one or two 20-mm guns with a .50-caliber machine-gun mounted in boats with only one 20-mm gun; two .30-caliber machine-guns and two 40-mm high velocity grenade launchers. The two .50 machine-guns were often seen placed in the forward turret when replacing a single 20-mm gun. Complement: 6 men.

Tet Offensive

From its earliest operations in the Rung Sat Special Zone, action by the MRF ranged far and wide over the Mekong Delta. The first major battle occurred between June 19 and 21, 1967 when the Army-Navy team trapped three Viet Cong companies about 15 miles south of Saigon and killed 255 communist troops.

Reacting to intelligence during July that two Viet Cong battalions were preparing to attack Dong Tam base, the Mobile Base ships weighed anchor, steamed 61 miles up river to a new site; and joined with Vietnamese Marine, Army and U.S. Army units in routing the surprised enemy.

The MRF recorded success of another sort in September when a landing and sweep operation in the eastern Rung Sat Special Zone uncovered a cache of 105 rifles and machine-guns, 165 grenades, 60 howitzer and mortar shells, and 56,000 rounds of small arms ammunition.

The MRF 1 launched a series of operations against the Viet Cong 1967-68 code-named 'Coronado'. During Coronado V in September 1967, the Viet Cong who had been adjusting to MRF tactics struck back with an ambush along a two-mile stretch of the Bai Rai River southeast of Saigon.

At the end of the four-hour engagement half of the vessels in the convoy had been hit by enemy fire; three sailors were dead and 77 wounded. Another six men were killed or wounded when the MRF operating with the South Vietnamese Army 7th Division succeeded in trapping elements of the Viet Cong 263d and 514th Main Force Battalions in October inflicting 173 casualties.

From October to the end of November 1967 the Mobile Riverine Force focused on reported troop concentrations north of the

Mekong between Sa Dec and Dong Tam, but the enemy avoided significant contact. Then on December 4th, the Viet Cong tripped an ambush against River Assault Division 112 on the Ruong Canal northeast of Sa Dec.

The boat crews turned the tables on the enemy on this occasion when they pressed on in spite of the deadly fire and landed the troops on the enemy flank. Soon other American and South Vietnamese combat units joined in the battle and 266 Viet Cong were killed and 321 small arms and 5,000 rounds of ammunition captured.

The actions of the MRF during the Tet Offensive of 1968 were the key to the allied military success in the Delta and earned the force the Presidential Unit Citation. The MRF was used as the primary reaction force in the Delta region. Its mobility and firepower were used most effectively against the NVA and VC.

The crew of a damaged ASPB return fire while attempts are made to plug up the holes and keep the boat afloat.

During the first week of February 1968, units of the 9th Infantry Division battled through the streets of My Tho and helped recapture the city. The troops then shifted to Vinh Long for several days of intense combat with three Viet Cong battalions. For the rest of the month the Army-Navy squad fought around the Delta's chief city Cam Tho. The force killed 644 of the enemy.

On the morning of April 4, the MRF launched a two battalion riverine and reconnaissance-in-force operation in the Truc Giang and Giong Trom district of Kien Hoa Province. RADs 91 and 92 lifted the infantry into the Truc Giang operating area; after a special task force had been established in its fire support role on the Cua Tieu River near My Tho.

Shortly after dawn the mobile riverine base, less APL 26, relocated from Dong Tam, and was escorted to an anchorage on the My Tho River five miles southeast of My Tho in order to provide close support for the impending operation.

Shortly after dawn the assault craft of RAD 92 with their troops encountered a vicious ambush from an enemy force of unknown size about four miles northeast of Ben Tre. The devastating attack occurred on the Be Lai River just as the boats were moving toward the beach and consisted of heavy rocket, recoilless rifle, automatic weapons and small arms fire.

The land bordering the river at this point was thick jungle with underbrush at the water's edge. The enemy fire came from heavily fortified and well-concealed bunkers within the maze. In spite of the intense enemy fire the riverine craft delivered a barrage of covering fire, as they landed the infantrymen.

One company of troops landed directly in front of several enemy bunkers and remained pinned down in that precarious position for the rest of the day. Since these troops were so close to the bunkers, it was not possible to give them supporting fire. Several naval craft were hit in the initial assault, one by an RPG-7 HEAT (high-explosive anti-tank) round which exploded in the coxswain's quarters.

As a result of the combat action on April 4th, 12 assault craft received various degrees of damage. The most extensive damage was inflicted on A-91-2 and A-92-4. A total of six RPG-7 rockets impacted against the two boats, three of which were direct hits on the gun mounts. One Monitor received a heat round that killed the captain and coxswain.

On April 6, after two days of vigorous fighting the MRF had a day of relative calm as they shifted the center of operations from the Bai Lai River to a point four miles southeast of Ben Tre. During the afternoon of April 7th, the infantrymen were withdrawn and returned to the MRB anchorage on the My Tho River; thereby terminating a very costly operation for the MRF.

In July and August 1968, the Mobile Riverine Force ranged throughout the Delta with its now full complement of river craft, support ships and 9th Division troops. In the latter month, the MRF joined with other U.S. Army and Navy units and with other Vietnamese forces in a large-scale penetration of the U Minh Forest, long a Viet Cong stronghold.

Although the enemy fiercely resisted this intrusion, inflicting heavy casualties on the allies, the campaign was pursued with thoroughness heralding subsequent similar operations to deny the communists security in the whole of the Delta area. Having demonstrated their work Task Force 117 were in the vanguard of the Delta campaign until the riverine assault force was disbanded.

Sealords

In late 1968, the Johnson administration realizing, after the Tet Offensive of February and March and the follow up attacks during the spring, that the allied military struggle was not faring well and conscious of the growing domestic opposition to the American role ordered the gradual withdrawal of U.S. Forces from Southeast Asia.

'Vietnamization' of the war was the cornerstone of American policy during the period 1968-1973. A new naval campaign was launched, however in October 1968, when the U.S. Navy was still at peak strength. SEALORDS (Southeast Asia-Lake, Ocean, River and Delta Strategy) program was designed as a concerted effort by U.S. Navy, South Vietnamese Navy, and allied ground forces to cut the enemy's supply lines from Cambodia and disrupt operations at their base deep in the Mekong Delta.

On August 25, 1969, all but one of the barracks ships were returned to the continental United States and decommissioned. The repair ships were taken over by the Naval Support Activity and dispensed throughout the Delta to support SEALORDS. The small boats of two river assault squadrons were turned over to the South Vietnam Navy.

The first phase of the campaign in 1968 was to form a double barrier using two parallel canals some 35 and 40 miles southeast of the border. The second was the removal of obstructions to navigation from major waterways to permit strike operations.

From mid-1969 the SEALORDS campaign was in the hands of the South Vietnamese Navy, Marines and Infantry and the action continued until after the American withdrawal in 1973 when the lack of new equipment and supplies forced the operations on the Cambodian border to close down.

Glossary

ARG/SLF	Amphibious Ready Group/ Special Landing Zone.
ARVN	Army of the Republic of South Vietnam.
ASPB	Assault Support patrol boat.
ATC	Armored troop carrier.
Brown Water Navy	Term for a river navy.
CCB	Command and communications boat.
Charlie	American nickname for Viet Cong.
CIDG	Civilian Indigenous Defense Group – friendly armed villagers
Divisions Navales D'assaut (dinassauts)	French naval assault river fleet.
EOD	Explosive ordnance disposal.
LCI	Landing craft, infantry.
LCM	Landing craft, medium.
LCVP	Landing craft, vehicle or personnel.
LSD	Floating base (dock).
LSSL	Landing craft, support, large.
LST	Landing ship, tank.
MACV	Military Assistance Command, Vietnam – the overall U.S. command structure in Vietnam.
MON	Monitor – river gunboat.
MRF	Mobile Riverine Force (Task Force 117).
MSB	Minesweeper.
NVA	North Vietnam Army.
PACV	Navy patrol air cushion vehicle.
PBR	River patrol boat.
RAD	River assault division.
RAG	River assault group.
SEALs	Sea-Air-Land commandos.
STAB	SEAL team assault boat.
Viet Cong	Communist guerrillas.

Index